ENDANGERED!

WOLVES

Casey Horton

Series Consultant: James G. Doherty
General Curator, The Bronx Zoo, New York

BENCHMARK BOOKS

MARSHALL CAVENDISH

NEW YORK

Benchmark Books
Marshall Cavendish Corporation
99 White Plains Road
Tarrytown, New York 10591-9001

Library of Congress Cataloging-in-Publication Data

Horton, Casey.
    Wolves / Casey Horton.
        p.   cm. — (Endangered!)
    Includes bibliographical references (p.   ) and index.
    Summary: Describes the appearance, habits, and behavior of wolves, their malignment throughout history, and the current danger of their extinction.
    ISBN 0-7614-0213-6
    1. Wolves—Juvenile literature.   2. Canidae—Juvenile literature.
3. Endangered species—Juvenile literature.   [1. Wolves.
2. Endangered species.]   I. Title.   II. Series: Horton, Casey. Endangered!
QL737.C22H67 1996
599.74'442—dc20   95-11080
                                      CIP
                                        AC

Printed in Hong Kong

PICTURE CREDITS

The publishers would like to thank the following for supplying the photographs used in this book: Ardea 25; Bruce Coleman 18, 19; Frank Lane Picture Agency (FLPA) FC, 2, 4, 5, 6, 8, 9, 10, 11, 16, 17, 20, 26, 27, 29, BC; FLPA/Sunset 12; Natural History Photographic Agency 13, 14, 15, 21, 28; Oxford Scientific Films 22, 23, 24.

Series created by Brown Packaging

Front cover: Gray wolf.
Title page: Maned wolf.
Back cover: Gray wolf.

Contents

Introduction

The gray wolf is the largest of all the wolves. It has few enemies besides people.

Wolves can seem fearsome because of their piercing, yellow eyes, sharp teeth, and blood-curdling howls. In fairy tales, they are always shown as wicked creatures. In fact, reports of wolves attacking people are very, very rare. Wolves feed on the animals around them and are some of the best, most intelligent hunters in the world.

Wolves have been on Earth for millions of years. During that time, many different kinds of wolves have existed. Some are now **extinct**. This came about because their **prey** died out or because they could not get used to big changes in the Earth's climate. Other wolves **adapted** and survived.

Today, four kinds of wolves remain and all are in danger, mainly because people have **persecuted** them. There are the true wolves: the gray wolf, the red wolf, and the Ethiopian wolf. There is also the maned wolf, which is slightly different from the true wolves but closely related to them. In this book, we will discover how wolves live and what is being done to keep them from disappearing forever.

The maned wolf has very long legs and a rather pointed face. In fact, some people call it the "red fox on stilts."

The gray wolf looks a bit like a German shepherd dog or a husky. In fact, all pet dogs are descended from the wolf – even little ones like Pekinese.

Gray Wolf

This is the animal most people think of when they hear the word "wolf." There are more gray wolves than any other kind, and they are found in more places. For these reasons, we will spend a little more time with the gray wolf than with the other three kinds.

Wolves belong to the group of **mammals** known as dogs. This group also includes foxes, jackals, and the **domesticated** dogs we keep as pets. The gray wolf has a large head, pointed ears, and a long **muzzle**. Its coat is usually grayish with brown-gray patches, but sometimes it is completely white or black. Males can measure almost 7 ft (2.1 m) from the end of the nose to the tip of their outstretched tail. They weigh 45-175 lb (20-80 kg).

Gray wolves live in Europe, Asia, and in North America, where they are found mostly in Alaska and Canada. In some parts of their **range**, they are given other names. In Asia, the gray wolf is sometimes called an Asian wolf or

Areas where the gray wolf can be found

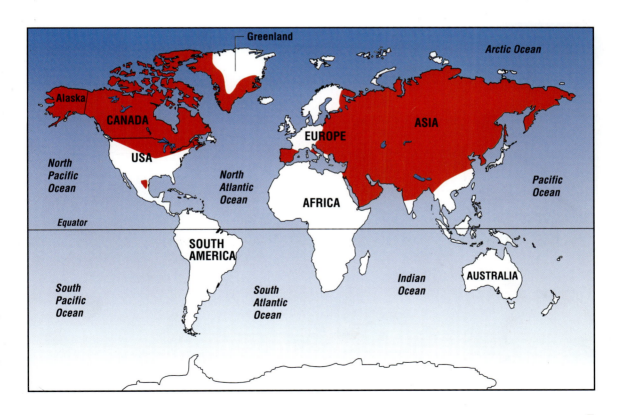

Gray Wolf

Tibetan wolf, whereas gray wolves that live in Europe are usually known as European wolves. North American gray wolves, meanwhile, are often known as timber wolves. Within their range, gray wolves make their homes in many different **habitats** – in forests, on prairies, on frozen northern plains, and in dry grasslands.

Gray wolves are **social** animals. They live in family groups called **packs**. A pack is usually made up of a male and female and their offspring. Gray wolves usually spend their lives with the pack they were born into. Sometimes a pack can contain more than 30 animals of various ages.

Gray wolves from the Far North often have white coats, which help them blend in with the snow. These wolves are sometimes called Arctic wolves.

A pack of gray wolves is led by the senior male. He is the strongest and probably the oldest of the males in the group. All the other wolves have their own special place in a pack – just as people do in a family. Sometimes a young male challenges the leader and tries to take his place. If the young wolf shows that he is stronger than the leader he will take charge of the pack. The old leader may leave the pack altogether. He becomes a lone wolf and must learn to survive on his own.

Gray wolves communicate with one another in a number of ways. They send messages by growling, yelping, or barking. But perhaps the best-known way in which wolves communicate is by howling. A pack of wolves often howls

Fights between the pack leader and a young challenger can be very violent. They sometimes lead to the death of one of the wolves.

together. Each wolf howls on a different note, which makes the pack sound a bit like a choir.

Another way in which wolves communicate with each other is through **body language**. For example, the leader of a pack will hold his tail straight up to show that he is in charge. He may also snarl and show his teeth if he is angry. Sometimes, if a larger, stronger wolf approaches a younger wolf, the younger wolf may lie down on the ground. By doing this, it is telling the stronger wolf that it does not want to challenge it. Many fights are avoided in this way.

Within a pack, usually only the leader and his **mate** – the senior female – have cubs. Gray wolves give birth in the early spring. The four to six cubs are born in a **den**, a safe

A group of European wolves howl in the snow. Sometimes a nearby pack will howl in reply.

place prepared by the mother. The newborns are deaf and blind, and are fed on their mother's milk. The cubs open their eyes after about two weeks and soon come out of the den for the first time. This causes great excitement in the pack, and all the wolves gather around to see the new cubs.

Besides feeding and sleeping, the cubs can now spend time playing. One of their favorite games is wrestling with one another. This is fun, but it also helps them work out how they will fit into the group. Playfighting teaches them how strong each of them is. The strongest usually take more senior positions in the pack.

At about two months old, the cubs start to take solid food. They cannot hunt for themselves yet but have food brought to them by other pack members. When the pack

A young wolf cub stands at the entrance to its den. A den is usually a hole dug in the ground by the mother. Sometimes, though, it may be another animal's hole or a cave.

returns from a hunt, the cubs go to each adult in turn begging for food. The adults do not refuse them. Wolf packs take great care of their cubs because they will be the only ones born that year. A pack must raise young wolves to replace the wolves that die or leave the pack. Otherwise it will grow smaller and eventually cease to exist. By the late summer, the cubs are able to go on short hunts. They follow an adult, but not necessarily a parent. By the fall, the cubs are expected to find food for themselves.

Gray wolves feed on a variety of small animals, including hares and beavers. They also eat much larger creatures, such as deer, elk, and moose. These are too big for a single wolf to overcome safely, so the pack works as a group to catch and kill prey of this sort.

Gray wolves have great endurance. A pack can travel up to 125 miles (200 km) in a day in search of food.

At the start of a hunt, the pack moves out in single file. Once they have discovered the tracks or scent of another animal, the wolves spread out and set off in pursuit. Sometimes, a single wolf chases after the prey, while the rest of the pack follows a little way behind. When the first wolf tires, another comes forward to take its place, and so on. In this way, a pack can keep up the chase until the prey is too tired to go any farther. Then the wolves attack.

Gray wolves once lived all over the northern half of the world. But people have been killing them for centuries. As

A timber wolf feeds on a white-tailed deer. Gray wolves have strong jaws and teeth that are made for tearing flesh and crunching bones.

a result, gray wolves have disappeared from parts of Asia and from most of Europe. The story has been the same in North America. Before European settlers reached the continent, about two million gray wolves lived in the area now covered by the United States (excluding Alaska and Hawaii). The settlers were afraid of these wild animals. They poisoned, shot, and trapped as many of them as they could. As people turned forests into farmlands, more and more wolves were pushed from their lands or killed. By the 1950s, there were only a few hundred gray wolves left.

Since then, **conservationists** and others have taken steps to save the gray wolf. It is illegal now in the United States for people to kill gray wolves, except in Alaska.

Besides being killed as pests, gray wolves are also hunted for sport and for their fur.

Conservationists have started special gray wolf programs, too. In Wyoming, wolves have been released into the wild in Yellowstone National Park. The government has even agreed to pay local farmers and ranchers if any of their farm animals are killed by these wolves. Meanwhile, in Minnesota a center has been set up to teach people about wolves. It is thought that if people understand wolves, they may treat them better in the future.

Because of these laws and programs, gray wolf numbers are rising, and wolves are returning to areas where they used to live. Gray wolves can now be found once again in Minnesota, Montana, and Idaho. However, many people still do not trust the gray wolf, and conservationists know that this skillful and intelligent hunter is still far from safe.

Although the gray wolf is still at risk, its future looks a little brighter now.

Area where the red wolf used to be found

The red wolf got its name from the reddish fur on its head, ears and legs.

Red Wolf

The red wolf is smaller than the gray wolf, larger than the coyote, and looks like a cross between the two. It measures 4 ft 4 in-5 ft 8 in (1.3-1.7 m) from the end of its nose to the tip of its tail and weighs 45-80 lb (20-36 kg). Red wolves are not red all over. Usually, their backs and sides are grayish with brown or reddish tinges, and the fur on the belly is pale or white. Their tails usually have a black tip.

Like gray wolves, red wolves are social animals and live in family groups, or packs. But while a gray wolf pack can easily have 30 members or more, a pack of reds never

contains even half that number. The reason for this is that red wolves do not stay with the pack for life as most grays do. Once they reach about two years old, red wolves leave their own family group and set off to start another. Until they meet a mate, they live as lone wolves.

Life as a lone red wolf is full of danger. Each pack of red wolves lives in a particular area of land known as a **territory**. So, when it leaves the family group, the young lone wolf leaves behind the safety of the territory as well.

One red wolf helps another to wash. Taking care of each other in this way strengthens the pair's relationship.

17

Red Wolf

Alone in the world and in new and strange surroundings, it must go in search of a territory of its own. As it roams, the lone wolf may come into contact with people and be shot, poisoned, or trapped. Or it may stray into the territory of another pack of red wolves.

Wolves mark their territory with their own special smell. They do this by spraying their urine on rocks, tree stumps, or fence posts that lie along the edge of the territory. If a strange wolf wanders into the area, it normally picks up the pack's scent and knows it does not belong there. Occasionally, though, a young wolf enters a rival territory by mistake. The owners will not stand for this. They will attack the intruder and may even kill it.

A red wolf makes its way through its forest home. The red wolf can also live in swamps and on coastal plains.

The red wolf lives only in the United States and is seriously endangered. At one time, it could be found as far north as Pennsylvania and as far west as central Texas. However, people persecuted the red wolf because they thought it was a threat to their cattle. Red wolves may attack young calves if these are not kept out of harm's way. Healthy adult cattle, though, are too big for them to kill.

As red wolf numbers fell, some red wolves bred with coyotes because they could no longer find mates of their own kind. The cubs that were born were half red wolf and half coyote. When these animals grew up, they in turn often bred with other red wolves, adding to the number of

At one time, anyone bringing in a red wolf skin to the authorities was paid money for it. This practice has now been stopped.

cubs that were not pure red wolves. This was not a problem for the coyotes because there were plenty of them all over the United States. For the red wolf it was a disaster. The population was already tiny, and too few pure wolves were being born to replace those that were dying.

In 1973, the United States government made it illegal to hunt the red wolf, but even this could not stop the fall in the animal's numbers. By 1980, there were no more pure red wolves left in the wild.

Fortunately, however, scientists had already taken a number of pure red wolves into **captivity** and started a breeding program. This was successful, and in 1987, eight red wolves were let loose in Alligator River National

In the 1970s, scientists caught all the red wolves they could for a breeding program. Out of 400 animals found, 17 were pure wolves like this one. The rest were part wolf and part coyote.

Wildlife Refuge in North Carolina. These animals have settled in happily and are breeding. In 1991, more red wolves were released in the Great Smoky Mountains National Park, Tennessee, where they come into contact with people and livestock. Conservationists are not yet sure if these wolves will be able to stay. Only time will tell if people and red wolves can live side by side once again.

Conservation workers in North Carolina fit a red wolf with a radio set so that they can track the animal's movements when they release it back into the wild.

Areas where the
Ethiopian wolf can
be found

*Like gray and
red wolves,
Ethiopian
wolves can
communicate
by howling.*

Ethiopian Wolf

Scientists used to think that this animal was a jackal or
even a fox, but they now believe that it is a small wolf. It
is about 4 ft (1.2 m) long from the nose to the tip of the tail
and weighs 15-33 lb (7-15 kg). This makes it about the
same size as a coyote. In color, though, it resembles the red
fox. Its head and back are reddish brown, while its throat,
chest, belly, and the insides of its legs are white. The tail is
very bushy and is black toward the tip.

The Ethiopian wolf is named after Ethiopia, the East African country in which it is found. Like other true wolves, Ethiopian wolves live in groups. These packs contain a number of adult males and females, along with young of all ages. Male Ethiopian wolves behave like most gray wolves and stay with the same pack throughout their entire lives. Females, like red wolves, leave their first family group when they are two years old. They then wander in search of another pack to join.

Like other true wolves, each Ethiopian pack occupies a territory that it defends against rival groups. Early each morning, the pack gathers to patrol the edges of the territory. As they go, the wolves check for strange scents that tell them if rival wolves have been there. Every so often, the pack stops to make new scent marks.

Ethiopian wolves live in highland grasslands in the Balé and Simien mountains of Ethiopia.

23

When the wolves return from patrol, it is time for them to start feeding. Though they live in groups, Ethiopian wolves may hunt alone. Their favorite food is a kind of African rat known as the grass or swamp rat, which is active during the day. Large numbers of these animals live together in mazes of underground burrows.

If they know that there are wolves in the area, the rats stay beneath the ground. Meanwhile, the wolves wander on the surface, watching and waiting. From time to time, a careless rat shows itself above ground. When it does, a hunting wolf sets off after it at lightning speed. The rat's only hope of escape is to beat the wolf to the nearest hole and dive down it. Even if it reaches a burrow, a grass rat is

An Ethiopian wolf chases a grass rat. With the wolf hot on its trail, the rat must run for its life, zigzagging as it goes.

not always safe. The wolf thrusts its muzzle down the hole after the rat and tries to dig it out.

Hunting the Ethiopian wolf is now against the law. But for many years, the wolf was killed for its fur and because people thought it attacked farm animals. This is one of the reasons that this wolf is in danger of becoming extinct.

Many of the remaining animals live in protected areas, such as the Balé Mountains National Park. However, it is believed that illegal hunting takes place, and this is very difficult to stop. To make matters worse, farmers' dogs may have come into contact with Ethiopian wolves and passed on diseases that can kill them. Domestic dogs may also be breeding with wolves, producing young that are half wolf, half dog. There may be only 500 pure Ethiopian wolves left in the wild.

An Ethiopian wolf at home in its territory. The Ethiopian wolf usually hunts by day. In parts of its range, though, it is active at night in order to avoid human hunters.

Areas where the maned wolf can be found

Maned Wolf

The maned wolf is not a true wolf. It is a separate kind of dog, although it is closely related to true wolves and foxes. People call it a wolf because it is big. It measures about 5 ft 6 in (1.7 m) from its nose to the end of its tail and weighs about 45 lb (20 kg). Its fur is yellowish red, and it has a shaggy mane, which gives the animal its name. The throat, chin, and tip of the tail are white.

Maned wolves are found only in South America, in parts of Argentina, Bolivia, Brazil, and Paraguay. They do not form packs. They live alone, making their homes in open grassland or in swampy areas.

Some people think that the maned wolf has magical powers. There is a legend in Brazil that it can kill a chicken just by looking at it.

Maned wolves hunt at night, feeding on small mammals, insects, reptiles, and birds. They hunt by quietly creeping up to their victim and then suddenly pouncing on it. Even though they have long legs, maned wolves are not very fast runners. Scientists believe that they developed long legs in order to see over the tall grass that covers much of the area in which they live. Maned wolves also eat plants, in particular sugar cane. Another favorite food is a type of fruit that local South American people call "wolf fruit" because wolves like it so much.

Maned wolves do not howl. Rather, they bark, whine, and yap, like many domestic dogs. They also growl when they are frightened or preparing to attack.

Like true wolves, maned wolves occupy territories, even though they live alone. Here, a maned wolf marks the edge of its territory by spraying urine.

The maned wolf is greatly at risk. In some areas of its range, South American farmers often burn the land to kill off wild plants before sowing their crops. Many animals that maned wolves hunt eat these wild plants. When the plants are burned, these animals have no food, and they starve to death. This in turn leaves the maned wolves without food and they, too, starve.

Farmers and ranchers also hunt and trap the wolf because they believe it is a threat to their animals. Maned wolves sometimes eat domestic chickens, but they do not attack sheep and cattle. Many countries have made it illegal to kill the maned wolf, but hunting still goes on.

A maned wolf searches for food. Unlike other wolves, maned wolves do not dig with their paws but with their teeth.

There are few wolves of any kind left, and those that remain are at risk. Many people fear and hate wolves, and would rather kill them than share their land with them. Today, conservationists are trying to teach people that they have little to fear from wolves. In some places, they have been successful and wolves are making a comeback. But there is still a long way to go before wolves can be taken off the danger list.

Young maned wolves are brown-gray in color. Only when they become adults do they have their beautiful yellowish red fur. Female maned wolves usually give birth to two large cubs.

Useful Addresses

For more information about wolves and how you can help protect them, contact these organizations:

National Wildlife Federation
1400 16th Street NW
Washington, D.C. 20036

The Sierra Club
730 Polk Street
San Francisco, CA 94109

The Wilderness Society
900 17th Street NW
Washington, D.C. 20036

U.S. Fish and Wildlife Service
Endangered Species and Habitat
Conservation
400 Arlington Square
18th and C Streets NW
Washington, D.C. 20240

World Wildlife Fund
1250 24th Street NW
Washington, D.C. 20037

World Wildlife Fund Canada
90 Eglinton Avenue East
Suite 504
Toronto
Ontario M4P 2Z7

Further Reading

Endangered Wildlife of the World (New York: Marshall Cavendish Corporation, 1993)

Gray Wolf, Red Wolf Dorothy Hinshaw Patent (New York: Clarion, 1990)

Macmillan Children's Guide to Endangered Animals Roger Few
  (New York: Macmillan, 1993)

Wildlife of the World (New York: Marshall Cavendish Corporation, 1994)

Wolves R.D. Lawrence (Boston: Little, Brown, 1994)

Wolves Emilie U. Lepthien (Chicago: Childrens Press, 1991)

Wolves Seymour Simon (New York: HarperCollins, 1993)

Wolves Tom Wopert (Milwaukee: Gareth Stevens, 1990)

Glossary

Adapt: To change in order to survive in new conditions.

Body language: The body movements that animals use to show their feelings.

Captivity: Confinement; for animals, usually in a cage or small area.

Conservationist (Kon-ser-VAY-shun-ist): A person who protects and preserves the Earth's natural resources, such as animals, plants, and soil.

Den: A hole or cave that an animal uses as its home.

Domesticated: Having been tamed by humans.

Extinct (Ex-TINKT): No longer living anywhere in the world.

Habitat: The place where an animal lives. For example, the Ethiopian wolf's habitat is highland grassland.

Mammal: A kind of animal that is warm-blooded and has a backbone. Most mammals are covered with fur or have hair.

Females have glands that produce milk to feed their young.

Mate: An animal's partner, with which it breeds.

Muzzle: The protruding part of an animal's face made up of the nose and jaws. Animals with muzzles include bears, dogs, and horses.

Pack: The name given to a group of wolves that live together.

Persecute (PER-see-kyoot): To treat in a cruel way, often for no good reason.

Prey: An animal that is hunted and eaten by another animal.

Range: The area in the world in which a particular kind of animal can be found.

Social: Living in a group.

Territory: The area of land in which an animal lives. Some animals, such as wolves, defend their territory against others of their own kind.

Index